ERRANT NIGHT

T0363211

ERRANT NIGHT

JERZY BEAUMONT

RECENT
WORK
PRESS

Errant Night
Recent Work Press
Canberra, Australia

Copyright © Jerzy Beaumont, 2021

ISBN: 9780645008999 (paperback)

A catalogue record for this
book is available from the
National Library of Australia

All rights reserved. This book is copyright. Except for private study, research, criticism or reviews as permitted under the Copyright Act, no part of this book may be reproduced, stored in a retrieval system, or transmitted in any form by any means without prior written permission. Enquiries should be addressed to the publisher.

Cover image: 'Bright "Evening Star" from Mars is Earth', NASA/JPL-Caltech/ MSSS/TAMU, 2014
Cover design: Recent Work Press
Set by Recent Work Press

recentworkpress.com

PL

For Clementine

Contents

PART ONE:
UNDER DARKER SKIES

1.

(Twinkling stars aren't special; just wasted energy warped by atmospheric fluctuations.)

2. a)

Canberrans talk about two things in winter: Seasonal Affective
Disorder and how grateful we'll be come summer. Next time; *this
time*. I have the sun in my bones. A craving for warmth unsatisfied
by tinder. Matches. Walter Burley Griffin designed incinerators.
And Canberra. The difference lies in the brickwork. Detail. Speak
of the archaeology of absence, and even the ash is disturbed. This
isn't a little Sydney or an outer-outer Melbourne. I'm a fire sign, a
greedy summer tan. But winter here is cold, getting colder.

2. b)

Everything is detail. I'm not dead, but my autopilot days are cold.
Functional. August's grey snow is mostly dust and routine. Speckled
milestones posted online. Melt away. I feel something, sometimes.
Tattoo needles. Scalding coffee. Hangovers. I taste almost every
meal consumed. I know I'm SAD, but depression is my heart's
armour. Rusted shut.

3.

In this economy? I don't stop until after dusk, bussing south in the dim and dark. Disembarking on the far side of everything gives me time to think. *Solvitur ambulando.* Scudding clouds set pace. Sharp air under lunar corona, and the stars above——are gone. The night sky stands empty. No, that's not quite true. Though Canopus shines bright, Alpha Centauri is gone, Regulus too. Venus and Mars look to The Lion's empty throne, sombre and distant. Wholesome Dipper is a welcome sight, and Orion's belt holds fast, but the Southern Cross is missing. Have our nationalist lights fled, or been spirited away? Scout's honour; without compass the heavens spin freewheeling before my eyes.

4. a)

An astrophysicist wrote in *The New York Times* that we're training ourselves to ignore the cosmos. Light pollution is a filter we internalise. Even accounting for blinders, I only count a hundred —and three—stars. Vertigo rushes; the ground lurches. Blood flows backwards and hair stands on end. Will I fall upwards and out into space without that celestial safety net? Will the dark crash down?

4. b)

I won't bow beneath a dead sky as olm in a cave. A blind thing that crawls, knowing no better. *I have to find the stars.* Place some calls, hang up before they answer. Pack the essentials; toothbrush, scroggin. Phone charger, clean underwear, and my meteorite fragment. From Jupiter's periphery to Campo del Cielo to Canberra. Further yet, if I have my way. If I need to bargain with celestial bodies, I pray my roommate will speak on my behalf.

5.

My spaceship hunches in the backyard like a vulture. My pride
and joy. Built from schematics found on Reddit, fresh paint
gleams cherry red (picture swollen summer fruit, not casino-
garish). I nearly broke the bank on components, but it flies like
a dream; graceful as a swallow with a Prius' fuel-economy. My
ark incorrigible; child of toil. Engines purr; gravity claws for
purchase. For a single crystalline moment we hang in the possible
like a breaching humpback. Then comes that thrumming punch!
Adrenaline flies under the radar, zipping over rooftops and
highways. Winding window down (crankshaft archaic) I lean
arm out to collect neon halos from street lights, fast food signs,
and front porches in a darned butterfly net. The trunk rattles; I've
brought all the spare bulbs from home, looting linen cupboard,
pantry, and kitchen's fourth drawer down. It's not enough. We'll
need more glittering understudies. Without stars, the fabric will
fall. I aim to pinion.

6. a)

I pluck unused indicators like grapes. Scan for glimmers, hunting light. Sweeping over lake top, we barrel-roll and skim starlight reflections from inky wash. (I'll put them back, I promise.) *It is not enough.* Breathe deep claustrophobes. Can you taste the deflating blanket-fort above? The crumpled airbag, the parachute pressing to Earth?

6. b)

GIO Stadium yields gold; a couple dozen HID lamps brighter than Fornax. I bank around suburbia as spotted vision clears, roll over Northbourne Avenue and harvest the lot. Blacken club scenes, plunge light rail into shadow. Pull fairy lights from City Walk's *platanus orientalis*, an angler's net flapping behind booster engines. (Oh, if the night fishermen could see me now! The cuttlefish coaxers and anglers bobbing for fry!) Yet it is still not enough, and the sky has tumbled to cloud height. Planes are grounded, pilots wheeze sick bag accordions.

7.

Engine idling outside hospital, I break into palliative care to
lift light from glassy eyes; diamonds from arthritic fingers. My
dedication wavers. I leave empty-handed (but for a few fluorescent
tubes). My ears pop as I slink back to cockpit. The pressure is
on. We need hope renewed, but at what cost? For all nobility of
purpose, I won't sink to psychopomp. It breaks my heart, but this
will have to do for now. It won't last. (The arrogance: of course there
is not enough luminescence on Earth to fill the heavens!) But it will
hold, at least until. Rise and cast substitutes out window, see them
puncture dark, flicker and stick. The sinking stops. Retreats. Halts
at the periphery of optimism.

8. a)

I circle back homeward, defiant in the face of true emptiness. An astrophysicist wrote in *The New York Times* that we don't want to see. I can't look away. If I call in sick, would you water my plants? Put the bins out early and step the fuck up? I pay my bills, tell loved ones I care. I do care, even at spiral's arm length. I won't be back until the night sky is flooded with light. Won't come home until my runway glows from Centauri to Sol; won't settle for anything less than the rightful state restored. I pack a lunch.

8. b)

I hate travelling, right up until departure. I suppose I hate the not-yet-travelling; the waiting, the suspended commitment to leap. This, though ... this feels right. As I break atmo', slipping tropo', strato' and meso' like oversized shirts, I feel a literal weight rise from my shoulders. Maybe it's the air pressure, or this growing distance from the cumulative anxiety of a planetful of stressers, but I feel it all the same. Grin and wave to Thermo', flip off Exo'—*I'll see you fuckers 'round!*

9.

I am not the religious kind, nor particularly patriotic, but there is something divinely inspiring about going to space. Or perhaps in leaving Earth. Gloved hand salutes each celestial body passed, mental recitation of Venusian trivia, Jupiter's storm, Neptune's everything. Pluto *is* a planet; this I can confirm. This cockpit is a private booth, all windows one-way mirrors. Yank wheel and barrel-roll to celebrate the orbits and ellipses; the nature of curved ascent and indirect progress and twisting axis and the heliosphere itself. I am ready to get ready. I punch through hydrogen wall, knuckles bleeding.

10. a)

Terrans have only one territory beyond our solar system. 4.24 light-years from home lies Proxima Centauri b. Barren, mostly. Terraforming was largely unsuccessful, but the lone triumph houses the port city of Narcissau. Located within a massive crater, Narcissau is an upended toybox; a cubist favela of imperma-housing and bolted on architectural addendums.

10. b)

Docks line the rim above, linked by spiralling wallbound shuttle to city floor. Narcissau buzzes as if a beehive in a cob loaf. To entrepreneurial dismay, extra-terrestrial life cared little for most trinkets of Earth. Most. They love our shipping containers. We learned to specialize without hubris. Traffic wholesale and hollow. Narcissau became the ironsided hub of trade. FIFO workers commuting across the void.

11.

The rumours about Narcissaun dockworkers are true; they're all bawdy drunks, but the shanties they bellow echo throughout the settlement. I have little to trade, but local humans pay well for nostalgia. I barter gaming consoles, books from my youth. I've memorized every passage, every quest. I give, and get all I need to trawl the still waters of deep space.

12. a)

I thought I had found a deserter. Abnormalities plucked from a deep space scan, but upon approach I discovered a planet bejewelled. Ablaze with not fire. Not-fire. Alighted. The surface was knee-deep in silicate bones. Opalised; the not-fire visible from space. I come from a land down under the boots of mining magnates and opportunistic narratives. Sanctioned piracy. Beauty in pressure. I drink vision, pay small change respects. Leave the dead to shine.

12. b)

Without regular use, the dust in my throat chokes and the hinges of my jaw squeak. My roommate is iron-stoic. Poor conversationalist. I wish I could say *I built an AI*, but I'm a lousy programmer. (I bought a kit online. Soldered on.) I don't crave conversation, but the dust accumulates. I'll admit to the dark outside that I treasure most the silence between pithy sparks. To name is to limit, so *Lexic Onthedash* will keep our relationship professional. Wired into the dashboard radiophone, tasked with trawling for pop hits and comm calls. *(What do you know, L.O., L.O.?)* Nobody calls. My number is a closely guarded secret. *('ello, 'ello?)*

13.

Travellers, do not take your eyes off the spaceroads, no matter how familiar the route. Debris litters the expanse. Near collisions are more common than you'd think. High Place Phenomenon is an unwelcome hitchhiker. Let hands remain at two and ten and *tight*.

14. a)

There are waystations, even in space. And, though the vents leak and the locals stare, there is something universal in the communal. There are no tables free in this rest-stop. A machine with porcelain face gestures for me to join them. They look like a ballerina in a music box, all wind-up grace and deeper machinations. I sit, and eat, and talk. The air is seeded with understanding. They ask me what I seek, and so I tell them. The food is cold and hard to touch, but melts upon consumption. I taste catfish, cut grass, halcyon days. My companion has input; I can see it pending.

14. b)

The food is cold, but I am not. Relishing discourse, I invite it. *Can you trap a* <**bird**> *by running at it* <**hands**> *outstretched? Can you take note of a half-thought in all its indeterminate by approaching directly? Remember a dream by snapping awake and leaping for* <**paper and pen**>*? No, you come at it from an angle. Like easing into a* <**swimming pool**>*, reversed. Sidle up to it, lash out at the last minute.* I have been chasing stars and found none to spare. Now I know why. The ballerina face is frozen, but the bodily shudders resemble mirth. They laugh at me. Me, my too-small ship. Myopic in the galactic expanse. I laugh too. There is a glow on the horizon of space. The centre of the galaxy pulses with light and life. I will journey forth, come at them sideways. The stars won't know I seek them until they're in my fist.

15.

NASA warns astronauts of space's radiation. Star-sailors and their glowing bones can sense solar winds' approach. Ripple sail. Billow so fine. Bones grow thin, muscles wither, but my vision is sharper than ever. There are supplements available at every waystation, on every inhabited planet but mine. My Medicare card is plastic. All these teeth are homegrown. I'll probably be fine. I have coping mechanisms. Met a therapist, once. (Did I tell you I quit drinking?)

16. a)

Back on Earth in a Chilean desert, the Atacama Large Millimeter/ Submillimeter Array (ALMA) focuses upon the spectrum between radio and infrared; a range known to sink and hide in water. Parched throats croak jubilant through cracked lips when ALMA found the H-dropouts; elder galaxies born in the first 2 billion years of universe. Galaxies so deeply buried in dust they defied detection 'til now. I pass one such senior. Cough plume, vent exhalation to mingle in offering.

16. b)

The sky of this world is blue; the grass green. Air is breathable, fauna both gentle and unafraid. There is bountiful good and the 'but' teeters at brink but never drops. Never bursts upon impact, to spray all with cynicism. The sky is familiar, and the grass is soft underfoot. This world is home to peoples of sentient sound. As they host me, I host them within my stories. Gather communities within my words. Though they are unversed in our language, the long-prescribed definitions, we share a joy. The resonance and boom, the hush and evocation. Drawn into lingua franca dances; the memorized stanza and flourish. If I ever emigrate beyond Earth, know that you will find me here.

17.

The typical composition of asteroids is not a sweeping remark one can make without courting inaccuracy. Many share the same base composite minerals—iron and nickel, carbon and craters. Common elements, found even in the frame and organs of spaceships. I will lead with this in later tellings of events, too ashamed to admit the truth outright. *I didn't see the raider ships until they opened fire upon me. Thought they were asteroids.*

18. a)

The hangar floor is cold. Vital heat burns deep within the station's core, but there are more important things than comfort. My ship is parked neatly, held down by gravlock boots. Ablaze. *Pirates* I tell the stationhands, looking at one another, extinguishers pending use. I won't let them douse. *Where I come from, a blazing ship is a funeral for kings.* I scoot closer and am warmed.

18. b)

Homeless in space. I cannot afford a new ship. The window reveals lethargic traffic beyond. I rest head to cool glass. A blue tie on Earth once recommended we let our parents buy us homes, if we cannot. My scowl needs no translation, yet it is my blue collar that fills coffers. Business is a universal language. A scrap merchant loans me a leaky junker to collect debris. To collect paycheck. Business is a universal ladder, and Time a parabolic investor. I was sent for old refuse, but found ancient relics. My boss retired rich – I took my cut and bought his ship. Towed the junker out to the system's edge and left it for the vultures to pick clean.

19.

I wish I could say *I built a new AI*, but I'm lousy with sentimentality. (Ripping *Lexic* from the pyre, we soldier on). I'd say what I want you to believe, but freely admit that you're too far to hear me. Call home and leave a message in white noise. Give number to ballerina grace. Nobody calls me back, but the means are out there. In safe hands. Pat my back. Buckle my belt. Shatter the crystalline in a static burst.

20. a)

As an outsider to every culture, I embody foreign. But this pilot-captain, hailer from *Trade Vessel Cilleuth*, knew both name and calling. They offer to sell me a rogue star chart; the journey paths of celestials unbound to any system. Unattached, these travellers could provide perfect alternative for absentees. The price? Prized. *('ello, L.O.)* AI crafted speaks to the crafters; the priorities and pitfalls of a species. With *Lexic* in hand, the captain could reverse-engineer a sapien understanding; a business model beyond the limits of finite Narcissau. Business is a universe unto itself. I hand companion over, feel solar winds strip the atmosphere away. Pull air from lungs—no. We're on board, and all air is cyclical. Perhaps I just can't breathe. *(L.O., goodbye.)*

20. b)

On the moon over (or under), I think I find a clue; a room without roof. Low atmosphere, vacuum bleeds in. There's a churning irritability within core; gaseous pressure vents oxygenated geysers. Keep the pressure on, breathe in deliberate recourse. Though it may take millennia, eventually this core will burn out. The dark will come rushing in. Have you ever heard an entire moon gasp for air? Would it happen all at once, or come sweeping across the horizon? The final wind to stir moondust? I don't know won't know. I will be long gone before then ... but in my dreams the breeze sweeps my footprints away.

21.

Scanned surveyance of world-upon-world from low orbit, storing data within ship's archive. When I check light-years later, I find tech corrupted, memory questionable. Unable to verify what was lost. Dizzying questions, burning up. Brittle concentration, laughter bubbling to lips for no-one to hear. I think I'm sick. My Medicare card is missing. I think maybe I had this coming. I spend a week with CO_2 farmers on a verdant moon. In exchange for wasted breath, they nurse me to health, showere me with gifts, promises of riches if I stay. They harvest thought with tech wizardry, spin data streams into visions. Substitutes of loved ones left on Earth. Supplicant sycophants called me *prime asset* and woo with acknowledgement. But the solar winds are coming. I can feel them in my loose teeth. The whole atmosphere will be ripped away in a howl, and I can't *can't* still. Sick.

22. a)

I stop. On an unnamed world in a barren system. Found a 'scape marred by an immeasurably vast sinkhole. Scans failed to locate the floor; probes never returned. Threw rocks in, never heard the splash. Perhaps it extends right into the mantle, or perhaps someone within caught cast stones. I don't know geology, but I do know hollow. Here I rest. Here I return to my best, my mostly-ok, my *ain't too bad*. She'll be right.

22. b)

I've never been to Coober Pedy, but every child of Oz is taught of the town's underground homes. Mineshaft mansions of sandstone, carved and cool. There is a manic energy to this fever; it comes in waves and title bouts. Lash out with pick. Break and shatter and haul heave hurl. It hurts. I think I've done in my everything. Don't tell mum. Destruction has always come so easily to these hands. White knuckle scars welcome red initiates. She'd be so disappointed. Can't you see I'm trying to make something of myself? *Harden up.* Haft bites into palm. Arms won't lift. Where I fall, a dugout stands. Sealant for the walls wounds words.

23.

I rest beneath topsoil. I want to stay, but a holiday without end is retirement. A farm upstate for old dogs of war. Pack absence into cargo hold. Leave dugout door locked. Depart from an unnamed world. Dissociate from unmanned system. Let bloodied dust be my flag.

24. a)

I can't keep this ship. It has seen me at my lowest. I can't recover my power over the machine. My inveterate sins become veteran war stories; I control the narrative, give morsels of wisdom to friends, employers, trustees. Indulgences bestowed. I risk nothing in the telling, gain microarrays of favour. But before this ship I was brought low. This human disgrace cannot be buffed out.

24. b)

In a limpet-like garage upon asteroid, I trade keys for keys, a hot meal and packed rations. The rock rotates slow. My new ship is just a machine. I will ride this medium to the end of convenience. Give no power but that which is drawn like taffy from spluttering engine. Transaction complete. Registered and non-momentous.

25.

I have seen a hundred thousand worlds since my convalescence. With every system jump, time hiccups back, and I arrive the day before I left. I am older than I look. I am the tired that endures. Countless wonders wash over me. I feel something, sometimes. I am the autopilot. A fleet follows me now; crewed by the accretion of worlds passed. I traded my ex-employer's ship in, up, on and on. I miss my first ship; nostalgia is a rare pang reminding me reminding *reminding* I was. I am what was. My latest vessel is a sleek whisper half a mile long, leaping solar systems under breath. All my teeth are anew. I am what was has become. I have climbed to the top without cheer. My hands quake but show no fault lines. I think I *think* I was looking for something. Opal bones. Rogue stars. What was now is. I come from a world of material fixation and incoherence.

26. a)

Where once I folded into cockpit, I now have flight deck. Galley, medbay. Empty. Luxurious captain's quarters. Bunks for a crew of twelve. All empty. Four cargo bays large enough to hangar pleasure craft. All empty. Dropship shuttles prepped and awaiting jettison. Flotsam is what you find adrift. Jetsam is what is discarded to drift. I am adrift; neither, both. But my hands know work, and the mechanical duress of creaking phalanges reacting to need drag me in their wake. Dust settles between the ridges of my fingerprints. Hands slide over golden railing, cold marble countertop. Rub thumb on arugula leaf in galley's hydroponic rig. Count to ten. These digits pry galaxies apart.

26. b)

Get a grip. Grip controls. Control controls. Under control. Mechanics of etymology. Cartilage 'tween calcium. Sinew and skin. Press to polycarbonate. Impulses firing electric. Get a grip. Maybe we're nearly somewhere, but that's superfluous. The most basic function of rockets is to go away.

27.

I cut engines, unmoored at the inner edge of habitable galaxy. Stare in at the inimitable bright, and know that it will never be mine. My phone rings. *There's been an accident—zrrt—Canberra Hospital—*

28. a)

Fall. Strike satellite. Plummet and rattle. A panel falls off a wing, slicing through the air as sycamore seed. A shuriken spiking Lake George's bed, to rest in silver glow and soil plume. I am a nosedive; an abrupt halt. A beautiful moon hangs over the turbines. I never did find my Medicare card. Never did find the light.

28. b)

The inner workings of hospitals are a maze. To hide the pain just around the bend, they add more corners. I keep bothering vital workers for directions. There was a typo on a laminated page at the last desk. I know this, but I can't remember words. Bold texted. *DOCUMMENTED*, I think. Something about catheters. There are a lot of wires in this body. From this body. Answers spike on screen and fall to linoleum. They bounce each time. Beeping rhythms respond from the bowels of the hall. I left shuttle double-parked. The fleet's in orbit; the stove is off. *Forgive me if this is a stupid question* asks young doctor of a nurse. Slow and methodical clarifications. Mundane in the midst. Midst of. This.

29.

It was cold outside. I'm wearing the wrong gloves. Rip them off, follow protocol. Text the family. Live tweeting journalist. Police raids. Wrong uniforms, all scrubbed up. Thickened heartvalve. Slurring. Beeping rhythms. Answers spike and fall. Beep bounce. Beep bounce. Beep bounce. Beep bounce. Beep bounce. It is so much easier (beep bounce) to show strength (beep bounce) for others. I've littered the heavens with junk. Placeholder mockeries. I don't know what to do.

30. a)

I pulled into my driveway, switched the engine off. Sat in the dark with ticking cooling engine. I did not know what to do. Reached for absent companion. Silent roommate. Star chart. Took phone instead. Scroll—saturate. *Too much.* Check calendar, pencil in grief from light-years away. I did not know how to feel. What to do. So I did what I tell others to do. I asked for help.

30. b)

You gave me your time. Your shoulder, your poems. I lay on the floor; you gave me your bed. Asked for nothing but tales of beyond here. I tell you of the cold vacuum. Dead worlds and the sooner-or-later-to-be. Tilt your head (remind me of fine-china grace) and ask askew: *all the nights without starlight. How many have you seen?* Countless. *Brother my brother, for every starless night, you have lived a day. Numb to the rays above, warmed only by purpose and blazing momentum, you have endured. Is it not enough to have lived all the betweens?*

31.

I did not know what to do, but I know I did something. Have done, will do. I disembark on the far side of everything behind me. *Solvitur ambulando.* I have walked this soil (and that of worlds unnamed). Dead stars glow at arm's length, and the living leave sometimes. I'm not there yet. My autopilot days are functional. Everything else is detail. In this economy? I don't stop until I'm done, riding home in the dim and dark. I wrote to *The New York Times*. Asked them to forward a message of appreciation to their astrophysicist. Swaddled meteorite freeloader in eggshell-white folds and too many stamps.

32. a)

Word rode in on a wavelength, months after returning to this darker Earth. Sitting somewhere between radio and infrared. *Lexic Onthedash. (What do you know, L.O.?)* They say *Trade Vessel Cilleuth's* passed a dark star site. Still occupied. They described something there, but the words came garbled: *eggshell to a furnace; an engine wrapped around a heart; a star inside a lockbox.*

32. b)

The astronomer Freeman Dyson envisioned Dyson Spheres; a cage and harness for a star's energy. I don't know if this shell is what Dyson dreamed of in '59, nor if this is an anomalous occurrence or the case for all the dark stars. But I do know this: work that goes unseen still burns with purpose. In purpose there is reason, and a reason for being can be enough. There are forces beyond my control. I renew my *NYT* subscription. Sent fleet to know. Reread the same article beneath a sky full of detritus. I remember sharing it with porcelain friend. They said *the stars don't tell us their plans.*

33.

(But gods... aren't they beautiful?)

PART TWO:
TRIALS OF NARCISSAU

1.

It has been fifty-four days since you died. I think about you a lot. Wonder how many stars count your absence at night. Some things can't be fixed.

2. a)

The Earth feels too close. I skim self-help articles. *How to function upon soil.* These granules churned by tectonics. Neighbours to the neighbours of your gravedirt's plot. The whole suburb whispers microcosmic. Australia burns. I jot *care* low on my to-do list, but an orange sky is hard to ignore. This season unbridled. Walter Burley Griffin designed a city hidden in smoke. My home. The distinction lies in the space between lips and filtration mask. The clues were sequestered in the betweens, but I have no time to find them. Can't see through the grey. Can't hear over soilsounds. Muzzled sympathies.

2. b)

I take flight sometimes to clear my head. Night flying. My eyes have adjusted to the grey nights; my lungs to eucalypt bonfire sediment. Fifty-five days ago ... had I called you, I would have said that maintenance and upkeep are king and counsel. One more day is one more day is one more day is *enough*. For today. For all the todays without collapse. With collapse, and repair. But some things can't be fixed. This you knew.

3.

Fifty-five days ago. Had you called, I would have phoned it in. This I know, and my mourning lulls and stuns in orchestral swings of shame. I am poor conductor. Tremolo nerves. I need distance from the din within. *Nessun Dorma*. I felt whole on a planet of song, but grief is a ragged chord. Rather than taint songfolk with misery, I head for Narcissau. I am greeted at the dock by sirens and extinguishers. My ship is fine; I brought the smoke with me. Confused fire wardens leave me be. This barren world is cold, but the city's engine heats all from below. Generators keep the air flowing. The gravity regulated. Artificial atmosphere intact. When the solar winds come, they go. I will stay.

4. a)

System-leapers like mine are megayachts of astronomical opulence, but I no longer need to cut the vastness of space. Just pick up groceries. Return to Earth. Eventually. I downgrade within the week. The dock above abode collapsed in the night. Stress. The house is fine. Freezer unthawed. But my ship was exposed. Rubble caught portside wing, flipped it into industrial generator. Fried spark triggered blast, all acrid smoke and exit.

4. b)

In this economy? Few can budget for surprises. I am lucky; I have ample reserves after downsizing. Flagship fetched a high price as rarity; a foreign build in a seller's market. Debris was taped off by safety wardens. I survey the carnage from porch and know; I could buy a new ship. There is so much temptation in *fresh start*. My spaceship lies beached under the weight of its own broken bones. It hurts to look at. Onlookers whisper and point. Judge themselves lucky. I could buy anew; be someone new. But bad things happen all the time, and resilience is *in* this season. I aim to rebuild.

5.

A spaceship is a highly complex network of co-dependent mechanisms. Any halfway decent ship is an ecosystem Amazonian in scale. This resurrection is a massive undertaking. Hard to encapsulate or capture in-frame. Focus down. Compartmentalise and cope. Breathe deep; move to be moving. I order parts online; read manuals for wisdom yet unearned. I have time and capital to spare. Today I am down, but I know *know* I know I'll know up again.

6. a)

I have friends in Narcissau. Pushed away. But the bones of this ship are laid out before me, flayed panels alongside. The enormity of the task ... I make my calls. In ancient arrangement, we trade homecooking and cold brews for welding and wrenchwork. The IKEA of it all. Watch them heft panes into place, mould rubber seals into joints, turn glass into windows. *They call this a barn raising,* I am told. By sundown the ship stands. Hollow reassurance.

6. b)

Parts ordered together. Delivered separately. Text message alerts. *We're here for you in this trying time.* I spend my days at work. I built an AI to help. Nothing fancy. It can't compare to *Lexic*, but I appreciate the company. All I had were scrapped parts Milo can and Cash's greatest hits. Me and my tin ear preacher get along just fine.

7.

The air filtration system is vital. Fortunately, it's not dissimilar to air-conditioning. Dehumidifiers. Easily acquired parts. Condenser fins and fan, compressor and capacitor. I weave filters from microfibre; hammer drip tray from tin. The booster rocket fuel lines are trickier. Still manageable. I think I'm starting to get the hang of this. Propulsion is just energy and conveniences, narrow channels to release. Vent and push away.

8. a)

Explosion in the night. Debris litters driveway expanse. *The fuel lines.* What was cobbled is now shattered. Scrapped mettle. *Fuck.*

8. b)

There are waystations in space, and Narcissau thrives upon transience. But with hangar space so expensive, I taxi shipshards to outskirts. Experience is a marketable resource. Free food a tremendous unifier. Across patties and snags I trade tidbits with local gearheads. They kick wheels, traffick sage advice. I offer onions. Choice of sauce. *Tomato or barbecue?* There is no wrong answer.

9.

Me, my broken-down ship. Packed away like Christmas. This hangar may be small and dirty, but at least it's cramped. The flatbed of all my shattering shares housing with an *aircraft*. How we have fallen. English Electric Lightning. Britain's old warhorse, out to pasture. To the relic's credit, it looks like it could taxi out. Take off. *Nessun Dorma*. Leaser shakes head; it's all body no heart. A chrome shell gutted for parts. I know the feeling.

10. a)

Tunnel vision. Obsessive efforts buried oh so deeply in dust circuitry and bated wallow. Messages accumulate; missed calls and clutter. I'm doing something important here. Tired of the ghosting, friends found me at home. Took me out of my house. My head. The typical composition of an apology is textbook. I promise to not drop out of touch again, even sound sincere. But this project has given me something to focus on besides death.

10. b)

Where I come from, a funeral is a wake is a celebration of life is a dirty word. I'm too tired to tell the truth outright. I tread barefoot upon shrapnel. I feel nothing.

11.

My mates take me out. *Leave the red flags at home.* There are no therapists on Narcissau. Only bartenders and echo chambers. We shoot the shit. Sink nepenthe shots. Tell tallmast tales of ships long passed. Banshee hotrods with ululating crystal engines. Of tin cans and bottle rockets. The Screaming Jets play on the juke. This is helping. Tonight, I feel *better.*

12. a)

I wake on friend's couch. Clothes laid out like a crime scene. I left something in the bar. A pent up howl. A bloodletting. Though hangxiety takes the wheel, I know I'll know better again. We cradle colour-coded electrolytes and nibble fats. Crackers. Salt. I make no excuses for my actions last night. *When in vino.*

12. b)

I walk home. Wince under light. Passing used shiplot, I wander in. Browse bruised vessels like a bibliophile to bookspines. Remembering tallmast tales, I wonder aloud about the chasm between *fresh start* and *repair*. Eavesdropping assistant leads me to the fixer-uppers. Tells me of home to build a rapport. A bond. Bridged. I'm on to something here.

13.

I strike gold in back. These ships; Cloudskimmer models. They house a quirk; a contextual novelty wrapped in refrasil heat shrouds. The particulate combustion auxiliary engine was never meant for much more than low-risk thrust perpetuation in polluted atmospheres. The scramjet engine vacuums smog, splits offending atoms at incredible heats for the push. It's what drew me to purchase. I can picture a blue sky and gleaming ship. I can picture happy. But I don't feel it. I'd rather burn detritus. Embrace grit. Ride with purpose.

14. a)

The Alcubierre spaceshift ensemble (with pneumatic actuator) is a game-changing component. The difference between aircraft and spacecraft is ambition. The height of vision. This tech raises eyes from clouds to the heavens beyond. Fire up spaceshifter and watch vacuum compress accordion, shrugging ship to port in a wrinkle. I could not buy replacement on Earth, nor stand local price-gouging, but sent word to *Trade Vessel Cilleuth* weeks ago. Package arrives, rip twined brown paper apart. It's the wrong size. I needed Model: T-062A, but get T-061E. Hurl box into wall, watch it shatter hiss and suck brickwork light-years away.

14. b)

I see fractal galaxies in the yawn. See strangers with my face in the fold. Sickened. Can't look away. Horror grows all elbows and claws and—snaps shut. I heave. I can't. Can't do this. Can't fake the okay, the same okay, the veneer of social palatability. Forget grave plot—I will bury us both in this bottle.

Break

15.

I am here. You left at low tide. I promised I wouldn't. I drank oceans; all on hand. I buy no more.

16. a)

I could have bought a brand-new ship, but gambled on repairs. I chose this path; perhaps I chose wrong. But I own that call. I yearn impatient for galactic expanse, but necessary steps have always been within reach. Each day further is a day won; even the narrow margins. The on-and-off-days, and the off-days, and those worse yet. I am not where I wish to be. Who I wish to be. But I will own that. I will patchwork my way to healthy enough.

16. b)

I once caught a ride in a medical transport. *The Asclepion* was Earth-sourced and rattled with Boeing familiarity. Bonesurgeons told of the deepest cuts—funding—and the marvels of empty-wallet ingenuity. The spaceship had airship organs. Picture EMT; wide grin and sandbagged eyes. *Whatever it takes, right? They don't ask* how, *they ask* where were you?

17.

The English Electric Lightning was the first British aircraft to exceed Mach 2; an unofficial world speed record holder, once. I have napped at Mach 2, but now I catch shuttles that ponder and crawl. Station to station. Hard plastic seats. I devour ego. Call leaser. Tell him I'll take my hangarmate; any other bird he finds. He has another aircraft across the lot. *I'm on my way.*

18. a)

The Fairchild A-10 Thunderbolt II is a cratered treasure. No; a ransacked temple. It's ok; I'm not here for the vestments and silver. I've come for the stone. Complete ships are damn hard to come by, but a barbecuer (two lamb snags in multigrain; tomato sauce and onions) has a matching set of booster engines sitting idle. He slaps barrel, hear drum boom proud. *The GE TF-34 Engines may sit like cigar stubs at the base of shipspine, but they've seen more airtime than us both. These boosters will bypass and bolster. Let history uplift you.*

18. b)

I take the Thunderbolt. Bastardised with the English Electric; with all salvaged parts on hand. The patchwork is an education. There is grace in fusion, between the thresholds of tolerance and embrace. With mates at my side, we finish the job together. It flies, but I am still bound to the shallows.

19.

The recycling hub may be the busiest market in town. What cannot be reused or stripped to base elements is atomised, but the rest clutters shelves tables and wire baskets in one glorious bazaar. My friends help me comb every damned stall, and between us we source a baker's dozen different Alcubierre spaceshifters—or parts thereof. We feed golden wire through ports, string each and all into an unbroken loop; a daisychain that feeds as it filters. I have helmed many ships, over incalculable distances. Time would hiccup back with every 'shifted leap, but as ever I seek to move forwards. I thought it a fair trade. I know better now. I learned something in the shattering. A sentiment I had to break to mosaic right. I cannot win for losing. Cannot be anchored in time, cannot flourish Pyrrhic. With this I will be freed from fixation past. Time marches on, and I step in beat. Unforgetting, but live and in colour.

20. a)

My first ship was little more than a perched view with chutzpah. My finest was an overcompensation; a bounty of comfort and numb. A wonder, apart. But this ship feels the most honest. Shipshards the most grounded. I run paintbrush flick between window and fuselage. Blow 'til lacrimal paint dries and think: *this one'll keep.*

20. b)

Months after fleeing, I depart for Earth. Twitch joystick, roll over space dust and shrink distance. It is not the avoidance of pain that will save me, but the dedication to repair. Fall; catch bounce moonlight off every polished dent and depression. Homebound, I dive for Earth. Canberra. Park in long-empty driveway.

21.

I turn the key. It pop hisses sparks and clunks off. Smoke wafts. Smile in the dark. I can fix this. (Tomorrow.)

PART THREE:
SOLVITUR

1.

It has been two hundred and two days since you died. I am on Earth. Canberra. The air is clear, the borders closed. The stars that left remain gone. If there are answers, I could not find them. I wish I could make a bold sweeping declaration. *If I cannot find them, I will become them.* Burn cold, shine hyperfocus bright. Turn all in reach to fuel. But that's not me.

2. a)

Had I wished to leave, for Narcissau or beyond, I could not. Lockdown is a lived state. We are to quarantine ourselves. Shoulder allostatic load and hunker down. Conversely, I feel too exposed in these bunker days. I have never lived through a pandemic before. If I am to stay, I need to become better at being.

2. b)

You had a big heart. A kindness to you. Left before the country burned and novel corona bloomed. I wonder; had you made it through that night, would you have made it to today? Tomorrow? I'll never know. A kindness, yet I am tired in a way whispered to the drowning and known to the drowned.

3.

Exhausted. I rest against ship's beaten panels, inert in driveway. I can't go anywhere. Wipe hands on jeans. Sip cold coffee. You had a big heart. I read that Dick Cheney has no pulse. System failure lead to surgery. His Left Ventricular Assist Device spins at 9,000 RPM. Never beats. If I am to stay, I need to become more. I research craftsmanship. Tissue rejection & biomechanical implants. The LVAD won't help me, but perhaps my future could be cyborg. Steel in my spine. I could become someone who can live in this world. Rebuilt to last a lifetime. Research——interrupted. Word rides in on an email from the United Nations' Office for Outer Space Affairs. Postmaster marked it spam, but the missive is clear. *I hope this finds you well.* In another lifetime, I sent fleet to know. To find the stars I could not. UNOOSA tells me my flock has come home to roost. They send rendezvous coordinates. We are free to clutter the sky over Saturn's moon, Titan. For a time. *Please see attached visa exemption.* My keys are in my hand before *Kindest regards.*

4. a)

Titan is the colour of dried blood. Eternally fogged by unbroken nitrogen obfuscation. Guided by orbital scans, I drop towards the UNOOSA base. Silver in the rust. Overshoot. I have never been to Saturn's moons before. With time to spare before the debrief, I blow past civil servants and out towards the bare and barren untouched. Lockdown has left me craving expansive horizons. Descend, taxi and halt. Exit cockpit. Walk a while. Bootprints in the sand.

4. b)

A day here is a fortnight on Earth. More. My mind is overcrowded. The landscape bare. Gravity lean. In this environment? I don't stop until after dusk, musing in the dim and dust. I need the time to think. *Solvitur ambulando.* Fleet of foot, I pass mountains of ice. Cryovolcanoes. Rivers and rivulets of liquid methane. Complex hydrocarbons. Deserts of red sand. Rippled dunes. Titan is ever overcast. I can't see the stars at all, but I've long learned to live with their absence.

5.

The first Earthborn to reach Titan's soil was the probe Huygen. Child of international collaboration. Borne by the Cassini satellite for seven years, Huygen filmed all it could. All the way down. Landed safe in a gully. Saw tumbled ice like Earthly riverstones. Pioneer's attention speaks to the ambitions of the curious; the priorities and pragmaticism of tempered dreams in motion. It took incalculable effort to reach this point, for rewards both rich and humble. Huygen fell through the atmosphere, and so we knew sky. Fell to riverbed, and so we knew of rivers. We named our first outpost after that probe. Shoulders of giants; we built the settlement of Huygen beside riverbed. Little worthwhile is achieved in a vacuum. Support, not selfish endeavour, is what brings us to wonder's door. Knock twice. Hat in hand.

6. a)

It takes an hour for the signal from here to reach Earth. Further yet to *Cilleuth*. I call *Lexic Onthedash*. We talk as I walk. Exchange scant few words over the miles. Titan is cold, but I am not. I tell old friend how I feel. Tell them my plans; of systemic overhaul and renovation. Wait all day for a reply. Cryovolcanoes rise burst and retire before crackled response reaches me. *Are you ready?* The fog of Titan blasts apart for the first time since creation. My fleet is here, backlit by Saturn's glow. In that frozen moment? I saw the future so clearly.

6. b)

I see it all. My self, remade to design specifications. Surgeons use my original bones, splice nerves to wire endings, ditch everything frayed. Keeping my father's eyes. Mother's cheekbones. Working with parts stripped from favoured spacecraft. I can see the ship-self of me. Becoming. Implant a second stilled heart, now willed to beat again. To share the burden. I look the same, though my hair is better. Double-tapping pulse. I have no ship. I am my vessel; panel beaten but whole. Hearts full. Yet with homegrown eyes I can see where this path leads. Life as a Sisyphean fixer-upper. Never settled nor satisfied. A lifetime of re-shed skin and *almost there*. Sooner or later, I will need to stop running. Need to accept the Here of it all. I see all this upon horizon, see the haze come rushing back in overhead, and cannot answer my friend.

7.

Schools of darting silver flashes. Flocks of hollow bones high above. Stretched leather shrieking in the dark. Every time I see fleet in motion, I am reminded of nature. It takes a Titanian month, but I visit every ship's captain for debriefing. Each wove narrative thread through the time between. Tales of lab-grown blackholes. Of deep space telescopes that fold distance and biodome terraformers. Eden under 'brella. Of shrewd dredgers that'll harvest *anything*; liquid metal from dead cores skimmed planetary rings and nebulas of excess. Of thousands of new species discovered. Of strange signals traced to graveyard outposts. Of pharaoh tomb vessels, corridors choked with would-be looter corpses. Of out-manoeuvring pirates in crowded asteroid fields to rescue hostage vessels, of repelling corsairs like circled wagons of old. Of hiding in dust clouds of vaporized asteroids and the stinging dunes of acid-washed beaches. Of a missed decimal causing 'shifter nav error, leaping bold and bright into primitive war, shocking them into ceasefire. I am told these tales.

8. a)

I am told these tales, and a quintillion more. This universe—all these things happened here, and more. I could chronicle without leave until heat death and still never capture all it contains. I am told of things I've never experienced—things I never will. The universe is so much larger than we can possibly know, but today—today I know more than yesterday. There must be a way, in this impossibly nuanced 'verse, to live a full life under a darker sky. I dissolve fleet; release ships from service. Bestowing vessels to captains and crew as severance boons, I leave Titan alone.

8. b)

I had a mission. Burned cold as Hell's permafrost, hyperfocused and bright with catalytic purpose. Turned all in reach to fuel, cared nothing for the smoke in my wake. But that's not me anymore. Growth comes for us all. Rarely upon invitation. You left at low tide, and I drowned for a time. Trod water for a time. It is not that I've learned to swim, nor found my way to shore. I feel the water at all times. The pressure, the crush, the current over under gills.

9.

It's near time to return to my world, but I am still without. Though ships have scattered, I took an Admiral's pension before retirement. No—a pirate king's cut. Business isn't universal at all. Value is subjective. Opportunistic and predatory. But the blessing of loved ones is a prize beyond. Friends a true boon. I felt better on Narcissau. I feel it again, and want to share this present. I phone ahead. Intercept *Trade Vessel Cilleuth* in the deep heat of the Horsehead Nebula. Venture aboard for a Titanian minute. Leave with lighter wallet. A weight off my shoulders. *('ello, L.O. You have been missed.)*

10. a)

I ride through the sky. Aglow. My world is not as cold as others. This I know. There is joy here among the living. I wish you could be here to see it, but flagellation in solidarity serves none. I may never live for happiness, but I don't need to chase euphoria, nor explanations. I am thankful to have known a night sky full of stars. Grateful to have known you at all.

10. b)

I still get tired. Still go out night flying sometimes. It feels good. I let myself feel good. It is autumn now. In Canberra, that means it is winter. Frigid air flows from mountaintops down into the valley bowl. Pockets as mist. Lace trimmed lawns. Lean out opened window. The crisp air on my face leaves me gasping. Remaining stars guide my flightpath. If there is a lesson to be shared, I cannot quantify or summarise it. I am still here. You are with me in all seasons. I weave through town, returning placeholders long borrowed. I never did find the stars, but I don't mind.

11.

I can see a path through the dark. My glowing bones light the way.

Afterword

My cousin took her life in September, 2019. She was twenty-one years old. At the time, I had been writing a manual of field-tested coping mechanisms, documenting and detailing how I had made it through my darkest years. How I became someone that I want to keep alive. I wanted to share these hard-won lessons with loved ones in pain. I wanted to share them with Clem. I took too long.

These words aren't perfect, but they're as honest and ardent as any I've crafted. I hope there is something within these pages that may provide small solace to others under darker skies.

Acknowledgements

This work wouldn't have been possible without the help of so many. My deepest gratitude goes to both personal supporters, and the titans of craft who have inspired *Errant Night's* content.

To Shane Strange and the Recent Work Press team; this has been a dream come true. To my editor Penelope Layland, for her patience, wizardry, and genuine appreciation for the words I was ever-doubting.

To all members of my family near and far: I love you, and understand if these pages are too heavy to lift.

Gratitude to Cassandra Atherton, Christopher Brown, Julia Buker, Marc Carlton, Aki Collins, Cat Cotsell, Arielle Cottingham, Nadine Davidoff, Es Foong, Abdulrahman Hammoud & The Dirty Thirty, Matt Harvey, Menno Hess, Paul Hetherington, Andrea 'Vocab' Sanderson, Sharifa Tartoussi, UC Writers, Brian Whelan, and the ACT Writers team. To the inimitable poetry community of Canberra; I owe so much of my growth to your example. To Alex & Moog, for their eleventh-hour aid. To James Catling & the Psycho Somatic Firestarters—thanks for making Large Space Mistakes™ with me.

One of the best aspects of works of this kind is deep-diving immersion in real science, and the fiction build upon it. This book would be a flimsy thing, if not for the prior efforts of the following giants:

Hello Games' *No Man's Sky*, James S. A. Corey's *The Expanse*, the generosity of NASA, Michio Kaku's *The Future of Humanity*, Massif Press' *Lancer RPG*, John D. Clarke's *Ignition! An Informal History of Liquid Rocket Propellants*, Richard Morgan's *Altered Carbon*, M.K. England's *The Disasters*, Jon Favreau's *The Mandalorian*, the United Nations Office for Outer Space Affairs, Miguel Alcubierre Moya, Freeman Dyson, and so many more.

From atop your shoulders I reach for these stars.

Finally: to Clementine. Thank you, for staying as long as you could.

Glossary

Allostatic load: The wear and tear upon one's body and mind, brought about by chronic stress.

Campo del Cielo: The Argentinean impact site for the meteorite by the same name. The Campo del Cielo meteorite is thought to have fallen to Earth over 4000 years ago, and may have originated from Jupiter's asteroid belt.

Canberra: The capital city of Australia, built upon Ngunnawal and Ngambri Country. Indigenous sovereignty was never ceded.

FIFO: Fly In Fly Out; workers who are flown into a worksite and provided with meals and lodgings for their time deployed.

Griffin, Walter Burley: The architect of the city of Canberra.

Lake George: Located approximately 40km north-east of Canberra, Lake George (or Weereewa by its traditional name) is typically dry, though it may hold water after abundant rainfall.

Medicare card: The mint-green registry card for those covered by Medicare, Australia's universal healthcare insurance system.

Nepenthe: A mythical drink, thought to soothe and bring relief from sorrows and grief.

Nessun Dorma: The highly renowned aria from Puccini's opera *Turandot*. Famously sung by Luciano Pavarotti, the title translates to 'Let no one sleep'.

Seasonal Affective Disorder (SAD): A mood disorder brought upon by seasonal changes, such as the diminishing of Vitamin D exposure in the shorter days of Winter.

Solar winds: The stream of plasma particles released from the Sun's upper atmosphere.

Solvitur Ambulando: Latin, lit. 'It is solved by walking'. To work out one's issues on a hike or while otherwise in motion.

Further Notes

The *New York Times* article referred to is 'Is The Evening Sky Doomed?' by Dr. Kelsey Johnson. It is available at: https://www.nytimes.com/2019/08/17/opinion/sunday/light-pollution.html

The Alcubierre spaceshift ensemble (with pneumatic actuator) is named after theoretical physicist Miguel Alcubierre Moya, in honour of his work on warp drive principles in the 1994 paper 'The warp drive: hyper-fast travel within general relativity'.

About the Author

Jerzy Beaumont is an Australian Anglo-Zulu poet and arts worker. His work has appeared in publications such as *Cicerone Journal, Australian Poetry Journal, The Dirty Thirty Anthology, BITE Magazine, The Canberra Times, Hobo Camp Review, Cordite, NO NEWS,* and more. He represented the ACT at the Australian Poetry Slam finals in 2017, and has performed his poetry throughout Australia and the USA.

In 2019, Jerzy stepped into the leadership role of Brisbane-based publishing house *Bareknuckle Books Pty Ltd* & associated *Bareknuckle Poet Journal of Letters.* This is his first book.

Printed in Australia
Ingram Content Group Australia Pty Ltd
AUHW020929220224
390784AU00002B/30

9 780645 008999